I0075949

Servant Leadership

90 Minute Guides

Michelle N. Halsey

Copyright © 2016 Silver City Publications & Training, L.L.C.

Silver City Publications & Training, L.L.C.
P.O. Box 1914
Nampa, ID 83653
https://www.silvercitypublications.com/shop/

All rights reserved.

ISBN-10: 1-64004-035-8
ISBN-13: 978-1-64004-035-9

Contents

Chapter 1 – What is Servant Leadership?

Servant leadership can seem like a contradicting term, but it is becoming a very popular tool in many businesses. Servant leadership is a philosophy that involves focusing on others (i.e. your employees), and focus on their success, and in turn build better professional relationships that can benefit both manager and employee. Servant leadership shows that managers can be great leaders while boosting their employee's confidence and further their success at the same time.

At the end of this tutorial, you should be able to:

- Define servant leadership

- Know the characteristics of servant leadership

- Recognize the barriers of servant leadership

- Learn to be a mentor and a motivator

- Practice self-reflection

What is Servant Leadership?

Servant leadership is a business philosophy that emphasizes the act of the leader, such as a manager or supervisor, focusing on the growth and development of their employees and ensuring their success. In doing so, the leader succeeds when their employees do. In a business team, servant leadership can not only help employees achieve and grow, but it can also benefit their leaders and the company as a whole.

A Desire to Serve

It is a leader's responsibility to guide their followers on the right path. But to become a better leader, it's not enough just to take the wheel and steer – you must also be willing to serve your followers and assist them in their own journey. A servant leader should have a desire to serve their employees, which includes taking the time to identify your employees and how they perform or being beside them as they face challenges. Take the time to assist in their growth and help them work toward achieving their goals. Don't be afraid to give yourself into their processes and become part of their evolvement.

Knowing to Share the Power

As a leader, it is a common feeling to absorb the 'power' of the position and a have a sense of superiority. But a servant leader does not save this power only for themselves because they learn to share it with their team of employees. Employees under a servant leader should feel some of the servant leader's power and pull, which can make them feel more empowered in their place on the team and in their own abilities. Sharing the power allows employees to feel like their contributions matter and that their input is valued.

Share the power by:

- Delegating

- Asking employee opinions

- Working together on challenges or projects

- Taking a census, when possible

Putting Others First

One of the main principles of servant leadership is the act of putting other's needs ahead of your own. As a leader, we can sometimes think in the 'ME' mentality and want to focus on our own agenda and needs. But in servant leadership, the leader must focus on his tea of employees first before focusing on themselves. The leader should focus on what the employee needs or wants, how they can achieve this and how it will make them successful in the long run. A leader should strive to develop relationships and even friendships with their employees and deliver feedback when possible. They must be able to set their own ego aside and realize that without their team of employees, no one can be successful.

Helping Employees Grow

Once again, as a leader, we can focus on our own goals, responsibilities and even our own challenges. But as a servant leader, the needs of the employee should come first and the main goal should be to help them succeed and grow in the company. A good leader knows that a chain is only as strong as its weakest link, so everyone benefits when every employee is encouraged, mentored and motivated. Sometimes this may mean you'll have to share in successes as well as failures, but every goal set and worked together is another stepping stone for the employee and helps them work toward their ultimate target.

Help employees grow by:

- Encourage goals

- Give feedback when possible

- Listen to their questions and requests

- Offer help but don't complete things for them

Chapter 2 – Leadership Practices

There are many different types of leaders and each one has a different method and approach to handling conflict and success. However, many leaders often blend different style types together in order to find the right mixture for their employees. A leader must be able to recognize their own characteristics and styles, as well as the employee's personality and attributes in order to determine what style of leadership will work best.

Democratic Leadership Style

Democratic leadership is a type of leadership that utilizes the input and opinions of the team as a whole, rather than just the opinions of a select few. Many decisions are often based on some sort of vote or census from the team and then discussed with everyone. Every team member is allowed to have their voice heard and give their thoughts regarding projects, job duties or general work environment. Employees will feel as though their input is valid and will feel more appreciated in their work. While the democratic leadership can be helpful in big groups, it can be difficult to navigate when making quick, immediate decisions or if a decision must be made against the group conformity.

Characteristics of democratic leadership:

- Uses voting practices

- Employees help shape decisions

- Employees feel more valued

- Not optimal for immediate decisions

Laissez-Faire Style

Loosely translated, laissez-faire is a French term that means 'allow to do'. It has grown into a work style that generally allows employees a lot of freedom to perform as they want in order to reach a goal or complete a task. Leaders can still provide support, advice or input if requested but will typically leave the employee to their own means. Many employees enjoy this type of freedom and work better when they feel as though they are not being watched. However, some employees need motivation or help with time management and may not function well in a laissez-faire environment. Also, employees that do not have the necessary knowledge or skills to complete the job will need more instruction from the manager and will require the leader to regain control of the team and become more active in leadership.

Characteristics of laissez-faire leadership:

- Allows a lot of freedom among employees

- Do not get involved in work flow

- Some employees may lack motivation

- Managers could lose control of the team

Leading by Example

As a leader, especially a servant leader, it is your responsibility to work to inspire your employees and encourage them to reach and succeed for more. One of the best ways you can do that is to show them the way – leading them by your example. Commonly known as "practice what you preach", when you lead by example, you demonstrate to your employees that their success is possible; you show them that they can achieve their goals and can strive for what they want. Employees will still need the guidance, motivation and even structure as they grow, so it's important that leaders still work alongside their employees and be accessible to them when needed.

To lead by example:

- Remember that employees look to you

- Inspire and motivate employees

- Give feedback – both positive and negative

Path-Goal Theory

The path-goal theory is a leadership theory written by Robert House that a leader should change their leadership style based on the situation at hand. It recognizes that not all employee or all problems are the same and may require different approaches. The path-goal theory not only focuses on how the leader can help lead their employees, but is also based on what the employees need/want, such as more structure, types of feedback or simply time to work on their own. This theory claims that the leader should want to help their employees identify and achieve their goals, assisting them along their growth path, and in the end offer rewards or incentives for their achievements; and in order to do so, the leader must be flexible in their approach and leadership style.

Types of leadership under the path-goal theory:

- Supportive leadership – focuses on building relationships

- Directive leadership – communicate tasks, goals, and expectations

- Participative leadership – work directly alongside your employees

- Achievement-orientated leadership – set goals and tasks for your team to complete

Share the Power

For some leaders, learning to share the power can be one of the hardest obstacles they face. After all, leaders are supposed to have a sense of power and use it when they can! But a servant leader knows that when they share the power with their employees, learn to be empathetic and share successes with employees, they in turn gain more power in the end and become an even better leader.

Being Empathetic

Being empathetic toward employees can seem like an easy concept, but many leaders actually do not practice empathy with their team, which can lead to unhappy employees. Empathy should not be confused with sympathy – empathy allows you to put yourself in someone else's shoes and see how they feel. By being empathetic, leaders are able to share the power by metaphorically getting on the employee's levels and understand the problems and challenges they face and how it affects the work they do. It shows the employee that their leader listens to their problems and recognize their efforts, which in turn can actually boost their confidence and create a desire to work harder for their leader.

Be more empathetic:

- Use active listening

- Understand personal challenges or obstacles

- Do not mistake empathy for weakness

Learn to Delegate

Many leaders have a problem with proper delegation. Many leaders fear delegating tasks because they fear the employee may not complete the task the right way, so the leader develops the old attitude that "if you want something done right, you've got to do it yourself". However, this type of thinking can be harmful to the servant leader and their team of employees. A leader must learn to delegate to not only ensure that they are not doing all of the work themselves, but delegating also instills a sense of trust among the employees when they know that their leader can trust them to do something right.

Tips for delegating:

- Assign the right task to the right person

- Give clear instructions

- Ensure understanding before releasing

- Follow up

Their Success is Your Success

This element of servant leadership is the easiest to comprehend: a leader knows that when their employees succeed, they succeed as well. There is no 'I' in team. Once again, a chain is only as strong as its weakest link, so if one link breaks, the whole chain falls apart. But if every link is strong and capable, then the chain can withstand almost anything. A leader must work with their employees by coaching them, guiding them, offering advice and help when needed in order to help them meet deadlines, achieve their goals and grow professionally. As employees succeed and become an asset to the company, leaders will feel the success as well because they will have the satisfaction of knowing that the employee reached success with their help and will continue to do great work under their guidance.

Know When to Step In

As a servant leader, it is a natural desire to want to serve our employees and to assist them in every challenge that they face. It's natural to want to hold their hand at times until they have finally reached their goal. But a leader must also know when they need to step back from the employee and when is the right time to step in and help. Employees should possess the right knowledge and skills to work a task or complete a project. Of course the employee will face challenges or have trouble in some area, but the employee must first try to work out the problem themselves. Although a leader may observe the employee and see when they are challenged, the leader must know that it is appropriate to stand back while the employee works through the problem. Only when the employee cannot progress further or is at a point in which they do not have any skills or knowledge of, the leader can step in and offer help or guidance. It can be a hard balance between letting the employee work on their own to learn more and doing everything with them every step of the way, but a servant leader can find an equilibrium somewhere in between and benefit both the employee and the leader.

Chapter 3 – Characteristics of a Servant Leader

There are many qualities and characteristics that define a servant leader, including good listening skills, empathy, power of persuasion and great communication skills. Although a servant leader may develop or follow different leadership styles, they must all possess some of these main qualities and characteristics in order to become a great servant leader to their employees.

Listening Skills

Great listening skills can be an important tool in any position. Leaders must be able to listen to their employees and actually hear what they are saying and what they are needing. Active listening is a common tool used in improving listening skills because it involves listening without distractions and then periodically repeating back what is heard for clarification. Good listening skills also include being able to remove distractions, never interrupting while someone is speaking, and paying attention to non-verbal communication, such as body language, tone and gestures. A servant leader knows that improving their listening skills can improve communication with employees, which in turn can lead to better professional relationships.

Improve your listening skills by:

- Actively listen

- Avoid interruption

- Give your undivided attention

- Notice non-verbal communication

Persuasive Powers

Some leaders confuse power and authority with the ability of persuasion. But persuasion is a powerful tool that can be used without, well, power. Persuasion is the art of using your knowledge and expertise in order to enlighten and encourage others. It does not use force or backhanded coercion. A servant leader can use persuasion to build unity among the team and conformity when making big decisions. Of course persuasion should always be back by facts and research, so a servant leader should never use persuasion that is based on false information or personal choices. Persuasion builds trust, so leaders must learn to use it effectively.

Help improve your powers of persuasion by:

- Know your facts and do your research

- Aim to educate

- Knowing when to listen to the other side

Recognizes Opportunities

Sometimes when a leader recognizes an opportunity for growth and expansion, it is often referred to as foresight. Generally, a servant leader can recognize an employee's potential or certain skill set and can see an opportunity for them to set a goal or complete a task. Sometimes the leader can simply observe how an employee works and find a good fit for them. Communicating with each employee allows the leader to get to know each employee and build a personal relationship with them. Other times, simple work evaluations can be done in which the leader takes notes about the employee and creates an outcome from their findings. Whatever tools the leader uses, it is always important to listen to their intuition as well and always keep their eyes open.

Common tools to identify opportunities:

- Observe the employee

- Keep open communication with employees

- Perform formal and informal evaluations

Relates to Employees

Being able to relate to an employee is similar to being able to be empathetic, but requires a little more emotional involvement. A leader should be able to relate to an employee by remembering how they got to the position they are in and what leader helped them along the way. Leaders can relate to their employees because they used to be one. When employees need help, or struggle with a task, their leader should be able to relate to their sense of need, rather than criticize or judge them for it. When it's time to delegate tasks, ensure that you are assigning duties and not barking orders or demands. Allow the employee to work on their own as much as possible and let them work on their own confidence level. In the end, employees will feel closer to your equal and less like just another one of your employees.

Chapter 4 – Barriers to Servant Leadership

We've covered a lot of qualities and characteristics that make a great servant leader, but it is just as important to recognize what can hinder someone as well. Servant leaders are meant to encourage growth and promote confidence in their employees, but delivering excessive criticism, demanding action from employees and simply refusing to engage with them can create the complete opposite effect.

Excessive Criticism

Constructive criticism can be a helpful tool in management when it is used correctly. However, simply delivering criticism to employees without any form of evaluation or redemption is damaging to the employee and the confidence they carry at work. Excessive criticism can cause employees to feel as though they cannot perform their job correctly on many levels, which can lead to a lack of confidence and decreased productivity. A servant leader should review any form of criticism before they deliver it to the employee and determine if it will ultimately be helpful to them and what is the best way to deliver the feedback so it is constructive – not destructive.

Think before delivering criticism:

- Is this helpful?

- Can it be worded more effectively?

- How will the employee perceive this?

- Can I offer any positive notes with it?

Doing Everything Yourself

Learning to delegate is an important step in becoming a great servant leader. When a leader delegates tasks (and not demand action), it shows their confidence in their employees that they will complete the job right without much interference from management. But when a leader decides to simply do every task by themselves, it can not only create a very large workload for them to do, but it loses the faith of the employees and can weaken professional relationships. As a servant leader, learn to delegate and assign tasks to avoid the workload 'burn out' and show faith and trust in your employee's abilities and skills.

Remember to delegate:

- Show trust in your employees

- Give clear instructions and expectations

- Give employees a chance to ask questions

- Follow up to ensure the task is completed

Sitting on the Sidelines

A servant leader knows when it is time to step in to help an employee and when it is the right time to step back and observe from a distance. However, if a leader constantly sits on the sidelines, refusing to participate and but still giving orders, they will lose the loyalty of their team and any respect as a leader. A servant leader is involved in their employee's successes and their challenges because they care about their achievements and growth. But a leader who simply sits on the sidelines and does not work alongside their employees shows that they only care about their own agendas and interests. By not participating in the workplace, this leader relays the message that they hold all the power themselves and have no problem telling their employees what to do, but won't actually put in much of their own effort. While employees may work for this type of leader for a short while, they will eventually feel unvalued and under-appreciated, leading them to move on to other areas.

Demanding from Employees

A servant leader knows how to delegate properly and make requests to employees without a sense of demand or threatening. However, many leaders feel that as a leader, they are entitled to demand what they need from their employees and expect them to blindly follow. A demanding leader will not only intimidate their employees to get what they want/need, but they will also demand more from them over time – such as more work to meet a deadline, more duties assigned to them to complete or more time spent at the office for various tasks. But this type of leader is actually not leading at all, but trying to build a herd of followers. Some employees may follow for the time being, but many employees will not tolerate all of the demands and seek to move on somewhere else.

Chapter 5 – Building a Team Community

A good leader knows that every member of the team brings a unique talent and aspect to the group. Every employee should work together and complement each other's skills in order to get work done efficiently. But a leader but also be aware of any challenges a team may face, such as clashing personalities, and be prepared to step in and remedy any situation.

Identify the Group Needs

The servant leader knows the purpose of their team and has most likely started defining goals for the group. However, it is important for the leader to also identify the needs of each group member and the group as a whole. Every member is different and every member needs something different from the leader. Some may need further coaching; some may need more independent work while others will simply need periodic feedback from management.

As a group, the needs may be a little more complex. The group will need to have some sort of goal or charter that defines what they are working toward. The group will need to establish what tools or supplies are needed and what days/hours will need to be worked to accomplish their deadline. Identifying the group needs can seem like one of the easier aspects of building a team, but if overlooked, it can weaken the foundation of the group and crumble before the project is finished.

Complement Member Skills

When building a team, it is important to identify every team member and what skills or talents they will bring to the group. Many teams often feature members that are good in various areas, such as bookkeeping, research, public speaking or presentations, so that each member can excel in their area while contributing to the whole team. Rather than have a few members try and handle all aspects of the project, bring on several members that can divide tasks and duties more evenly and will work best as a group. One the leader has gathered all of the team members for the group; it's important to start building relationships among members, so try using some team building activities or begins a Questions and Answers session.

Common team building exercises:

- Great Egg Drop

- Survival Scenario

- Two Truths and a Lie

- The Great Escape

Create Group Goals

Essentially, the group goal should outline why the team was created and what ultimately needs to be done. Once your team or group is assembled, one of the main tasks is to create goals that the whole group can work toward. They can be work oriented, such as setting productivity goals or ultimate deadlines, or can be goals based on group members, such as working together to finish a subproject or goals that aim toward allowing members to get to know each other. The group goal should be created with every member in mind and should include input from each member. Goals that are created together are achieved together.

Tips for created group goals:

- Determine what the ultimate outcome needs to be

- Identify every member's part in the goal

- Take input and opinions from every member

- Create a charter or outline for everyone to see

Encourage Communication

Communication can be a scary thing for newly built teams, or even teams with new members. It is important for a leader to not only encourage communication among team members, but with leaders and management as well. To increase communication among members, encourage employees to get to know one another and build a working relationship. Employees that are more comfortable with each other will communicate better. For leaders and management, host small meetings or gathering to speak with teammates and allow them to give their ideas and inputs, or just talk about problems they are having. Let employees know how to reach you so they can communicate with you when needed. Encourage communication in any way possible so that employees always know how to reach each other and their leaders.

Tips for encouraging communication:

- Welcome input and opinions from team members

- Encourage team members to build relationships

- Schedule small, regular meetings or gatherings

- Stay in contact – whether by phone, email, text, etc.

Be a Motivator

Motivation is an important tool to use in the workplace because it keeps employees uplifted and inspired to keep moving forward. But every employee responds to different methods of motivations, so the leader must be able to know what makes their employees tick and what works for them. Employees work best in an environment where their feel their leader is behind hem and gives them a good reason to do great work.

Make it Challenging

It can be difficult for a leader to make the workplace a challenge because they may not be aware of what their employees can handle at one time. But a servant leader should be aware of the term 'grow or go' that is often used in the workplace. 'Grow and go' is a concept that means if a team leader or other management does not challenge the employee or make a stimulating workplace (i.e. 'grow'), the employee may 'go' elsewhere. This could mean they leave the company entirely, or it can refer to their sense of confidence and willingness to work. A servant leader can help keep the workplace interesting by helping the employee grow in their own area, as well as others, by allowing them to expand their job duties or take on additional projects. Never feel threatened by those that want to take on more, but welcome the challenge they seek in new opportunities.

Provide Resources

Sometimes the simplest form of motivation is ensuring the employee has everything they need to succeed. This can refer to physical resources, such as supplies, team members or training materials. Resources can also include personal support, such as encouragement and feedback. After all, employees cannot do their job right if they do not have all the resources that they need. As a leader, let your team know that you are a valuable resource they can use, especially if they need something they cannot acquire on their own.

Common types of resource to provide:

• Physical supplies, such as paper, pen, computers, scanners, etc.

• Additional training materials or class time

• Emotional support and encouragement

• Coworker and other management support teams

Ask for Employee Input

Sometimes a leader can struggle with finding ways to motivate their employees, but the simple solution is to just ask the employees what they want. Seek out the employee's input on various topics, such as how they like to be rewarded, what drives them to do better, or simply ask what their leader can do to make their job easier. Most employees are eager to share what make them happy and will feel valued while giving their thoughts and opinions. Now that the leader knows what makes their employees happy and productive, they can use the information find better ways of keeping them motivated.

Methods of gaining employee input:

• Add a suggestion box

• Hold open discussion meetings

• Invite employees for one-on-one sessions

Offer Incentives

Bonus and incentive programs are a popular motivation tool for many employees. Incentives can come in many forms, such as monetary bonuses, gifts, special titles or even manager recognition. Some employees may not respond to certain types of incentives, so a leader should recognize different forms of incentives and know which ones are best for their team. It is important to know the difference between an incentive and a bribe for good work. Employees want to feel rewarded for the work they have not – not like they are being coerced with a small gift to work harder.

Tips creating incentive ideas:

- Determine what forms of incentives motivate the team

- Gain employee input about existing incentive programs

- Develop clear performance goals for all employees

Chapter 6 – Be a Mentor

Being a mentor can sometimes be lost in terms such as 'manager' or even 'coach', but mentors are a valuable tool to many workplaces. Mentors can be helpful to new employees or to employees who have begun to lose confidence in their work. A good leader must also take on this mentor role and ensure their employees are getting the boost they may need.

Establish Goals

One of the best tools a mentor can give their employee is the ability to establish and set goals for themselves. Start by asking the employee what they want to achieve and how they want to reach it. Individual goals can include work issues, such as increased productivity or decreased distractions, or can be more personal, such as working to decrease personal absences. When working with a team, leaders should ensure each member has their own set of goals, and then establish goals for the team as a whole. This ensures that everyone has a goal to work toward on their own, as well as a goal to work with the rest of the team. Goals help everyone stay focused and can make them feel valued as an individual and as a group.

Tips for helping set goals:

- Ask the employee what they want to achieve

- Outline a path that can help get them there (there may be more than one)

- Determine a reward or incentive for when the goal is reached

Know When to Praise or Criticize

As a leader and a mentor, it can be difficult when to determine an employee should be criticized or reprimanded, or when open praise will be an effective tool. Praise and compliments are a great tool for building confidence in employees, but too much can lose its luster. Employees that are over praised may begin to lose faith in what their mentor is saying and lose the desire to work hard for that well earned praise. On the other hand, employees that are over criticized or chastised may lose self-confidence and pride in their work, causing them to create more errors and low productivity.

Praise and negativity should be based on the individual employee, not the group. If you must criticize, always do so in private and use phrases that are not personal attacks. With every negative point, offer a positive note as well to counterbalance. Let the employee know that you are there to help them, not attack them. Additionally, use praise and kudos when an employee has shown a change in their productivity, such as meeting a goal or over-succeeding on a quota. Do not use praises for everyday tasks and accomplishments or they will lose their value and will no longer feel like something special.

Create a Supportive Environment

In order to mentor and bring together a team of employees, a leader must be able to create a supportive environment for them to work in. After all, employees do not want to feel like the workplace is a place that should be feared and only generates criticism or humiliation. A servant leader should act as a mentor by creating an environment that is safe and supportive to employees, where they do not fear you or other employees. Visit with employees periodically and build a sense of comfort and trust so that communication is always open. Let employees know you are available if they need you and take the time to speak with them if you are approached. Your employees will appreciate the support and in turn will feel confident that they are not alone in the office.

Benefits of a creating a supportive environment:

- Employees are happier working together

- Employees feel comfortable approaching you with their problems or ideas

- Employees are more receptive to feedback

Create an Open Door Policy

Whether you are mentoring a new employee or an entire new group, one of the first things to establish is an open door policy for the office. Let your employees know they can come to you with any problems or concerns they are having – or even with positive ideas they want to share. Seeing someone as a leader can be intimidating or downright scary, so assure employees that you are there for them and want to support them in their goals and challenges. Give them ways to reach out to you, whether it in your office, by phone or by email, but also establish simple boundaries, such as best times to contact or following a chain of command with management. Your employees will value your time and feel as though you are there for them – not just for the job.

Tips for creating an open door policy:

- Ensure everyone is aware of the policy

- Be open to listen to the employees and their needs.

- Always be approachable – avoid becoming too distant.

- Establish boundaries that allow employees to reach you, but by appropriate means/times

Chapter 7 – Training Future Leaders

As a servant leader, one of the best qualities you can possess is the ability to instill servant leadership into another leader. Training future leaders takes many processes and cannot be completed overnight. Take the time to teach great values for a leader, such as a desire to serve, the ability to be empathetic, and the knowledge of how to motivate employees.

Offer Guidance and Advice

It can be very frightening and intimidating for a leader in training to begin to learn all they need to know to become a great servant leader. The amount of information and training can feel overwhelming and make the trainee question if the decision is right for them. But as their leader and their trainer, it is up to you to help them through these challenges and help them achieve their goal. Offer guidance when needed and give advice on areas they may not be familiar with yet. This can include training materials they can take with them, personal one-on-one time or even personal advice that you found helpful. Share stories of when you were training to be a leader and let them know that you are empathetic to their needs. Sharing personal experience can be a great ice breaker and it lets your trainee know that you've been where they are now.

Identify Their Skill Sets

When training future leaders, one aspect of their training is to identify their skill sets and what talents they possess. While basic leadership skills, such as organization, strategic thinking, and problem solving skills, are necessary for a leader in training, it is also important to identify other skill sets they may also possess to enhance their leadership. Many candidates possess skills sets such as enhanced sales abilities, great communication skills, extended computer knowledge or good public speaking skills. The training leader should take the time to identify these skills in their trainee, which can be done in several different methods, including formal evaluations, direct observations, or simply speaking with the trainee one-on-one.

Methods of Feedback

Feedback is a very important tool during training. Not only will the trainee learn to receive feedback and gain knowledge about how they are doing, but they will learn how to give feedback to others and use when they are a leader on their own. Provide feedback to the trainee as they learn and let them know what areas they are excelling in and which areas need more work. Give praise when appropriate and allow time to set goals and targets. When training on how to deliver feedback, go over several different methods of feedback, such as informal versus informal methods, and tools that can be used in the process, such as surveys or evaluations. Different methods of feedback can be effective on different types of people, so it is important to know the different ways of delivering feedback so it can have the most effect.

Common types of feedback:

- Formal vs. informal

- Employee evaluation

- Feedback sandwich – using both negative and positive feedback

- The 3x3 method – utilizing three pieces of feedback in one

Establish Long Term Goals

When leaders are first brought onto a team or training area, one of the first things they do is establish a goal. Typically, these goals are short term, such as a goal to during their training session or a goal to achieve in the next few months after training. But when training future leaders, it is important for them to be able to set goals that are long term and require more time and work to achieve. Together, the trainer and trainee should establish long term goals and outline ways that goal can be reached within a certain amount of time. The goal should be realistic and reachable. Outline milestones and progress points you want to see while they work toward the goal. Of course, let your trainee know that you are there to help them when needed and your door is open to them. Remind them that they are not going to have to go on their path all alone.

Tips for making long term goals:

- Establish what the trainee wants to accomplish

- Set a realistic time frame

- Outline progress points or milestones to reach

- Schedule periodic meetings to check on their status and progress

Chapter 8 – Self Reflection

When the day is done and the employees have gone home, where does that leave you – the servant leader? While it is important to take care of your employees and help them grow to succeed, you cannot forget to help yourself grow and pay attention to what you want to gain or achieve. A servant leader has to have a desire to serve not only others, but themselves.

Keep a Journal

It may sound elementary, but keeping a journal of your goals, desires, progress and even current projects can not only be therapeutic, but can help you keep track of where you've been, where you are at now, and what you want to reach in the future. It can be a great tool for tracking different ideas, opinions or general feelings during training or working with employees. Don't be afraid to record any problems or frustrations you may be facing because the goal is to obtain honest self-reflection. Makes notes of areas you are doing well in and identify areas in which you think need more work. While you may be training and teaching others, don't forget to take the time to note your own challenges and achievements.

Types of journals:

- Handwritten or paper journals

- Web blogs

- Audio journals

Identify Your Strengths and Weaknesses

You spend all day evaluating your employees and future leaders to determine their strengths and skills and what areas they need more help with. But have you ever stopped to evaluate yourself? As a servant leader, it is important for you to identify your own strengths and weaknesses. Of course you have common leadership traits, but what other strengths do you bring to the table? On the other hand, what are your weaknesses that you need to address? What areas do you need to request help with? A good tool for this exercise is a simple written evaluation of yourself, but you can also use formal job assessments that identify job strengths and weaknesses, and of course a one-on-one conversation with a colleague can be a real eye opener.

The goal of this exercise is to be honest with ourselves. We cannot gain knowledge or seek help if we do not identify that there is a problem. If there is an area we excel in and identify as a strength, don't be afraid to 'hone' those skills and share them with others.

Identify Your Needs

A servant leader has the desire to serve their employees and help them in their areas of need. But a leader cannot forget to identify their own needs as well. Sometimes we have to admit when we are in need of something and not be afraid to seek help. You may be a leader, but you are not invincible. Maybe you need more help developing training courses? Maybe you need more help learning computer programs? Or maybe you just need help getting the office organized or in order. Some needs may be more personal, such as a need for personal growth or a need for some time to yourself. Whatever your need turns out to be, it is important to not bury them inside and try to solve them all yourself. Don't be afraid to reach out to others and request help with meeting your own needs.

Creating Your Own Goals

As a leader, one of the first exercises you stress to employees is to establish goals for them to work toward. This practice is the same for you. When you begin a new segment at work, whether it is training a group of leaders or creating a new team to work with, you should take the time to create goals of your own to work on. Periodically check in on these goals to see if you are moving on the right path or identify areas you still need to work toward. Don't be afraid to create long term goals as well that may take more time to accomplish. When you finish, determine if you can achieve these goals on your own or if you will need help from an outside source to do so. Don't be afraid to reach out to others for help achieving your own goals and desires.

Tips for creating your own goals:

- Make them realistic

- Make goals for work and for personal life

- Set tentative timelines

- Identify if you will need help in certain areas to reach your goals

The 90 Minute Guide series of books covers a variety of general business skills and are intended to be completed in 90 minutes or less. It is an effective way for building your skill set and can be used to acquire professional development units needed by project managers and other industries to maintain their certification. For the availability of titles please see

https://www.silvercitypublications.com/shop/.

No. 1 - Appreciative Inquiry

No. 2 - Assertiveness and Self Control

No. 3 - Attention Management

No. 4 - Body Language Basics

No. 5 - Business Acumen

No. 6 - Business and Etiquette

No. 7 - Change Management

No. 8 - Coaching and Mentoring

No. 9 - Communications Strategies

No. 10 - Conflict Resolution

No. 11 - Creative Problem Solving

No. 12 - Delivering Constructive Criticism

No. 13 - Developing Creativity

No. 14 - Developing Emotional Intelligence

No. 15 - Developing Interpersonal Skills

No. 16 - Developing Social Intelligence

No. 17 - Employee Motivation

No. 18 - Facilitation Skills

No. 19 - Goal Setting and Getting Things Done

No. 20 - Knowledge Management Fundamentals

No. 21 - Leadership and Influence

No. 22 - Lean Process and Six Sigma Basics

No. 23 - Managing Anger

No. 24 - Meeting Management

No. 25 - Negotiation Skills

No. 26 - Networking Inside a Company

No. 27 - Networking Outside a Company

No. 28 - Office Politics for Managers

No. 29 - Organizational Skills

No. 30 - Performance Management

No. 31 - Presentation Skills

No. 32 - Public Speaking

No. 33 - Servant Leadership

www.ingramcontent.com/pod-product-compliance
Lightning Source LLC
Chambersburg PA
CBHW071436200326
41520CB00014B/3722